# A
# Commitment
# to
# Greatness

RICHARD J. MAHONEY

# Table of contents

"Every

calling

is

great

when

greatly

pursued."

Oliver Wendell Holmes, Jr.

# Where we stand

Anybody who has been watching Monsanto for the past few years knows we have undergone one of the greatest changes ever experienced by a company of our size. We have sold off or closed down businesses with sales of more than $4 billion. We have drastically restructured the others, and seen them begin to grow again. We have spent $3 billion to buy or create new businesses. We have dramatically decentralized Monsanto to push greater authority and responsibility down to the scene of the action — the operating units.

The interim report is in. We're nearing completion in the transformation of Monsanto from a predominantly commodity chemical company, with two-thirds of its sales in the United States, to a broad-based international corporation with a powerful orientation toward high-technology products. This transformation offers the potential of superior returns for all who hold a stake in the company.

Such sweeping change cannot help but produce a degree of confusion, uncertainty and some pain. Several thousand Monsanto people either left with the businesses that were sold or opted to take early retirement. Many of those who remained found themselves in new positions with different responsibilities — sometimes enthusiastically, sometimes not. Not surprisingly, some people from the old Monsanto wondered what life would be like in the "new." The newcomers at Searle and NutraSweet, by contrast, wondered what their future would be under the Monsanto banner.

The expression of those concerns reaches me in a number of ways when I meet regularly with employees from all levels of the company to find out what is on their minds and to let them know what is on mine. Those meetings result in a barrage of questions that cover the spectrum of corporate life, but they tend to break down into four dominant themes.

> ■ *Why did we have to change? Wasn't the old Monsanto good enough?*
> ■ *There have been a lot of changes and upsets. When will we finish?*
> ■ *What will the new Monsanto be? And will I have an opportunity in it?*
> ■ *In the past, we were bound together by a common heritage and technology. What unifies this new Monsanto?*

I've written this book for all of our employees around the world in order to discuss and to attempt to provide answers to these and other questions. I also believe it is essential that you know the reasons behind the corporate goal that you have heard and read about: *To develop Monsanto into one of the great industrial companies of the world.*

That goal is as difficult to achieve as it is easy to state. But we should not settle for less with our vision of what Monsanto and its people can achieve in the challenging

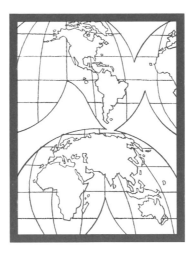

times to come — times that will test companies as they have rarely been tested before.

The Board of Directors and your corporate management have little doubt that Monsanto can become great. The strategy is in place, and it is already beginning to work.

What is my definition of a great company? It's simple! One that is *financially* among the handful of the very best and, importantly, *behaves* in the manner of the very best.

The key measure of greatness, partly because it makes all the others possible, is superb financial results, year in and year out. Pick any publicly owned company that you consider great and you will find that it boasts very healthy financial returns. Yet money is not the single measure of a company or its managers. I, for one, would hate to have as my sole business epitaph that "the company he served as chief executive officer generated superb financial results — but little else."

Financial performance is the "enabler" to greatness. To be truly great, a company must merit that title from a varied group of stake holders: its employees, customers and the communities in which it operates. Only by committing ourselves to the highest social, ethical and moral standards — along with financial results — can Monsanto achieve and maintain such a reputation. That is why a large segment of this book is devoted to the consideration of those *nonfinancial commitments* to greatness.

This book reflects both the belief that we can make Monsanto the best at what we choose to do and a determined commitment to make it happen.

So consider these words my personal invitation to you, the 50,000 members of the worldwide Monsanto family, to help realize the dream. After all, we all have financial and career stakes in the success of this strategy. And working for a winner is so much more rewarding — indeed more fun — than laboring in the middle of the pack.

A strategy is only as great as the people who carry it out. Together we can make Monsanto great.

"Even if
you are on
the right
track,
you'll get
run over
if you
just sit
there."

Will Rogers

# Why good was not good enough

In order to understand where we are today, and where we are going, it's essential to understand what made all this change necessary.

The decision to transform Monsanto was not made casually. Our world was changing. We could have done some necessary tinkering and simply fought it out with our traditional industry rivals and the major oil and petrochemical companies that now dominate much of the chemical industry. It is, after all, far easier to polish than it is to remake. Indeed, several other companies chose this route.

But we decided to remake the company.

Let me recount the thinking that led to the extensive corporate reshaping that has played so large a part in all our lives for the past few years.

To understand the plan we must understand the powerful forces that have changed the chemical industry in recent decades.

In the early years, from John Queeny's beginning, Monsanto was a bulk chemical supplier to the pharmaceutical and related industries. The company grew rapidly in the 1930s with the invention of polymerization technology and the availability of low-cost petrochemicals left over from oil refining.

Following World War II, Monsanto, like so many U.S. chemical companies, benefited mightily from two developments — the virtual elimination of powerful foreign competitors and the huge demand created by postwar reconstruction efforts. We moved strongly into plastics, fibers and the whole array of synthetic materials that replaced such natural products as soap, wood, paper, cotton and wool. Indeed, fibers accounted for well over half our total profits for many years. We even bought an oil company, refined the product into chemical raw materials and made high-volume products from them.

The continuing low price of oil permitted the chemical industry to remain *the* growth industry of the world throughout the '50s and '60s. Wall Street loved us. Monsanto's shares often sold at multiples of the stock market averages during the early 1960s. The only real mistake management could make was not to expand fast enough.

Naturally, this high profitability attracted competition. By the late '60s, the major oil companies and oil-producing countries were moving in on the traditional chemical industry by acquiring world-class technology — once our private province — and building plants to upgrade the petrochemicals they had been "giving away" to Monsanto and other chemical converters.

Before long, such previously profitable Monsanto businesses as plastics and fertilizers became low-profit centers. This was unwelcome news, because Monsanto's income depended on them. Still, the market kept growing for most of our products and there was, seemingly, room for everyone.

The oil shock of 1973-1974 further fueled this optimism by creating product shortages that allowed chemical companies to raise their prices substantially. The resulting flow of cash, coupled with the continuing shortages, triggered massive capital expenditures. For the first and only time in its history, Monsanto in 1974 exceeded a 20 percent return on shareholders' equity. Those were good times.

By the end of the decade, however, the world economy had slowed to a crawl. Forecasts suggested that the market for traditional chemicals would expand no faster than the gross national product of the developed world and a few developing countries, a dismaying drop from multiples of that GNP rate. And it would probably be the late '80s before demand could "grow into" the new production capacity built in the 1970s — and then only for a few years before the expansion cycle started once again, with its inevitable over-capacity.

As we looked forward from the 1970s, we saw in our product line a number of very profitable specialty chemicals. But the reality was that OPEC and the oil companies had forever changed the economics of the basic chemical industry — a major part of Monsanto. The once cheap hydrocarbons were no longer cheap. Whereas Monsanto once took 10 cents' worth of oil or gas hydrocarbons and added 30 cents' worth of technology, we were faced with buying 30-cent hydrocarbons and selling a finished product into a marketplace that allowed us to add only 10 cents of our technology. The value we added was dwindling — a guaranteed recipe for disaster.

Traditionally, the chemical industry had "invented" its way out of trouble. But we seemed to have already wrung the big-volume materials from the basic chemical building blocks. Indeed, no major new chemical families of products have come along in fields of interest to Monsanto since the early 1960s. No new basic fibers, for example, have been invented for at least two decades. Of course, there have been important inventions of single compounds, such as *Roundup* herbicide or aspartame, or product modifications, such as *StainBlocker* carpet fiber, but no entire groups of materials that we could exploit.

Coincidental with these events was the emerging concern in our society for a safe, healthy world. This issue hit the chemical industry head on. Many in Monsanto, particularly, will remember the stunning impact upon the company of Rachel Carson's books decrying the chemical harm to the environment. Managers who previously focused on products and profits suddenly had to think about regulatory strategies and cope with a flood of government requirements. We also had to make significant new investments toward the cost of cleaning up sites and dumps established in times when environmental standards were far lower.

Faced with the combination of a dramatically changed environment and unattractive prospects for a significant portion of our traditional businesses, management and the Board of Directors set out to reassess Monsanto's future. The three-pronged concept we employed is one I have stated often in Monsanto:

- *Stop doing what you can't do well.*
- *Do better what you do well.*
- *Start some new things for renewal and growth.*

Most important, do all these things simultaneously — not sequentially.

This exercise led to a set of conclusions that, when approved by the Monsanto Board of Directors and acted upon by employees around the world, moved Monsanto from a company often dependent upon events beyond its control to one that has a substantial say in its own destiny.

Let's examine what happened.

## Stop doing what you can't do well

We left those commodity chemicals businesses in which our competitive position was both inadequate and unfixable and where the future promised little improvement. We left them not because our people didn't know how to run them, but because they didn't fit our long-range strategy. Between 1980 and 1987, we sold or shut down $4 billion worth of businesses, ranging from our basic oil and gas exploration operations with most of their derivative chemicals, to businesses involving other products like polystyrene plastics, where our market position was inadequate. When we began, 30 percent of our assets were in commodity petrochemical businesses. As of this writing, the figure is about 2 percent.

Commodity chemicals can be rewarding for those companies willing to invest massive capital sums for highly cyclical returns — or for companies or countries seeking an upgrading of their basic raw materials. Neither of these applies to Monsanto, so we steered a course toward higher-margin, higher-value products.

## Do better what you do well

We realized that our problem areas were masking some absolute business gems. One thing I have learned over 25 years of managing is that people tend to concentrate on the problems that demand immediate attention. As one business writer said, "We spend so much time on those things that are urgent that we have none left to spend on those that are important." In that kind of environment, good businesses are permitted to slip to fair, and the fair to decline to poor. With the problem areas removed, our people at all levels were able to concentrate on bringing out the full luster of the gems.

Just two examples of many:

The fibers business was now able to focus its time and energies upon the bright prospects for nylon carpet fiber and *Acrilan* acrylic in the United States. It withdrew from an overcrowded market for both nylon and acrylics in Europe and from the bottomless demands of a badly outclassed polyester fibers business in the United States. The result: In 1987, fibers were star performers for Monsanto; they had been a loss in 1980.

Similarly, the surviving plastics operations became ABS, nylon resins and an emerging business in engineered polyblends. ABS, for one, was transformed from a money loser in 1980 to a solid performer in 1987 by focusing on the basics: quality, customer service, cost and product development.

During this period, cash from the sale of assets was "banked" for step three.

## Start some new things
## for renewal and growth

We looked across Monsanto for products, either existent or in developmental stages, that would respond to

accelerated development. We sank more funds into research and development programs, especially in plant and animal sciences and human health. We examined growth opportunities through acquisitions in several fields related to our existing skill base. Specialty chemicals, instruments, membrane separations and diagnostics were candidates.

As we moved through these exercises, we began to think about long-term goals for the new Monsanto.

As part of that effort, we examined our standing with

those groups that held the largest stakes in Monsanto — employees, communities in which we operate, customers and shareowners. We scored well for the wages and bene fits we paid, the working environment we provided and our behavior toward neighbors. And we also scored very well in our treatment of the people in businesses we had gone out of. The customer review was less consistent. Monsanto products were a mixed bag — top of the line in many areas, run of the mill in some. The shareowner review, as reflected in our stock price, was so-so. Financially, we were in the middle of the pack: solid and honest triers, but definitely unglamorous. If Monsanto had been a student, the report card would have read: "Good, but could do better."

We asked ourselves two questions: Why not aim to become the very best we could be? Why not target Monsanto to become a truly superior company — one of the handful of great industrial enterprises in the world? That way offered our best chance to produce superb rewards for all our stake holders.

We began to examine the characteristics of the leading companies — the IBMs, Mercks, and the like — and to review our prospects of joining that elite group.

The resulting analysis showed that one consistent tangible measure of companies regarded as great is the health of their bottom line. The great companies achieve sustained annual returns on shareowners' investment (net income divided by shareowners' equity) of more than 20 percent — and persistent annual growth in income of 10 percent. The key word here is *persistent*. The corporate stars achieve these performances virtually every year, regardless of economic fluctuations.

The stock market rewards these companies' current performance and future predictability by assessing their stock at better than twice the value of their underlying assets, or book value. The real achievers enjoy a stock market-to-book value multiple of four or more. At the time, Monsanto's return on shareowners' equity was 10 percent and its stock sold about at its book value of $40 to $50 per share.

So what were our prospects of joining the elite? To do so we needed Chemicals, Agriculture and Fisher Controls performing at the top of their industries, and silicon at least turning a profit. Not easy, but doable. But we also needed a major new component to add another source of significant growth to our company.

The strategy to make Monsanto a great company grew out of those needs:

■ On the chemicals side, we focused our efforts on those specialty businesses where we enjoyed technological and cost advantages over our competitors and could therefore realize superior profit margins. These included *Saflex* interlayer, high-performing plastics and resins, nylon and acrylic fibers, detergent materials, rubber chemicals, and specialty chemicals and materials. Taken together, these businesses became a powerful competitive force. The result: In 1986 and 1987 and into 1988, as I write this, the restructured Monsanto chemical unit is among the most profitable in the world.

■ In agriculture, *Roundup* and *Lasso* herbicides flourished, thanks to an intensive marketing push. But we had run dry on new products. We infused more research and development funds into this group, focusing initially on the plant growth regulators (PGRs), because of early success with our *Polaris* sugar cane ripener. PGRs turned out to be a poor bet, but other research in pesticides and plant sciences and the subsequent development of products to improve the efficiency of dairy and pork production using biotechnology were extremely promising. We also looked for supporting acquisitions. In the meantime, income increased significantly, largely on the strength of newly developed forms of *Roundup* and marketing programs for that great product.

■ Fisher Controls expanded its franchise beyond the energy field and moved into the forefront of the world trend toward factory automation with the *PROVOX* instrumentation system. Fisher instituted a three-part strategy — instruments to measure factory processes, valves to control them, and *PRO-VOX* to manage the whole system. Internal developments were to be supplemented by acquisitions of small and medium-size companies to fill the gaps in our technology.

■ The troubled silicon operations were trimmed into shape to survive the recession enveloping the electronics business and to be poised to break into the black when better times arrived and long-term direction could be better determined.

And we moved to add a major new unit capable of generating high returns on a reliable basis.

The most exciting, entirely "new" prospect for Monsanto was the science of biotechnology. Simply put, biotechnology can permit scientists to custom-design products for a specific need; they no longer have to screen thousands of chemical compounds in an attempt to find something that works. It's more precise and more predictable.

Our R&D work in plant and animal sciences for the Agriculture group convinced us of Monsanto's potential for successfully marrying biology to our chemical heritage. The opportunity was at least equal to that created by the petrochemical revolution of the 1930s — and without that era's reliance upon oil.

These insights led management to make every effort to position Monsanto at the forefront of the new technology. We invested both directly and through our venture capital efforts in the start-up of Genentech, Genex, Biogen and other pioneers in the biotech field. We boosted our research capacity with a $150 million investment in the Chesterfield Village Life Sciences Laboratory, and we hired Dr. Howard Schneiderman, a leading biological scientist, to direct our efforts. He initiated the hiring of top scientific talent and helped to forge strong links with researchers at Washington University in St. Louis and Oxford University in England, among others. These efforts began to result in exciting progress.

Our newly developed corporate financial target and solid progress on the biotech front caused us to redouble our long-standing interest in acquiring a drug company. For years, we had been attracted to the idea of moving into pharmaceuticals to add a profitable, noncyclical business to our corporate portfolio. But this had remained little more than a good idea. Now, we realized it was *imperative* to acquire such a company to serve as a major outlet for health care discoveries emanating from our biotech efforts and to provide a significant portion of our income targets.

Monsanto lacked the major skills to develop, make and sell the results of our increasing capability in pharmaceutical research. So we started a health care division with a mandate to get us ready to make a major acquisition, partly financed by funds husbanded from the sale of assets.

The payoff came in 1985. After several unsuccessful runs at G.D. Searle & Co., we finally acquired the Chicago-based drug company for $2.8 billion. The price was high, but the company was worth it. We got both the pharmaceuticals operations we coveted and an expanding stream of earnings from *NutraSweet* sweetener that could help to see us through the potentially lean years before corporate restructuring began to pay off. NutraSweet also brought with it the market and R&D seeds for an enduring business.

The target then was set to build consistently toward achieving a 20 percent return on shareowners' equity in the early to mid-1990s, and thereafter to achieve it year after year.

A 20 percent return on equity is not the only mark of

greatness. It is, however, the enabler, the achievement that makes everything else possible. Financial returns of that magnitude permit Monsanto to reward all its stake holders:

> ■ *We can attract and retain the best and brightest people and reward them accordingly.*
> ■ *We can provide the safest, most up-to-date equipment.*
> ■ *We can contribute more aggressively to enrich the communities in which we operate.*
> ■ *We can invest money in R&D toward discovery of breakthrough products.*
> ■ *We can improve our prospects of remaining free and independent to pursue the strategy that keeps Monsanto great.*

In the course of reshaping Monsanto and pursuing a pharmaceutical company, management gave a great deal of thought to the subject of a unifying corporate purpose. After all, we were wreaking massive change on a venerable institution and affecting the lives of thousands of people, many of whom took early retirement or left Monsanto with the businesses that were sold. With them went much experience and corporate memory. Some who remained wondered what had happened to the old Monsanto culture with its perceived "cradle-to-grave" employment and semi-paternalistic attitudes.

Those perceptions may always have been more myth than reality, but they were deeply ingrained in the corporate culture. When it became clear that many long-time employees would have to leave, I said to Bob Berra, head of personnel programs and public affairs for Monsanto, that we were only going to do this sort of massive change once in a lifetime, so we had to make sure we did it right. The retirement packages were as generous as we could make them. We hired the best counseling and outplacement people in the business to help laid-off workers find new jobs. There is no perfect way to do this difficult job, but we did our best to respect people's dignity and their past contributions.

When a company undergoes major change, that change must have a purpose — otherwise the vision is blurred, the upset intolerable. We knew what the old Monsanto was: proudly Midwestern in culture and temperament — trustworthy, ethical, socially responsible, generally accommodating, perhaps a bit insular. We were chemical-based, slipping a bit on the innovative front, and definitely manufacturing-driven. And for a company that had once been run "on the back of an envelope," we had become highly analytical — sometimes in the extreme — and often overly bureaucratic. All this we knew. So we set about redefining the "new" Monsanto and its values as a series of commitments. They go beyond the numbers to the heart of Monsanto, and they are an inseparable part of a great company.

"The trouble

with

opportunity

is that it

always

comes

disguised

as

hard work."


Anonymous

# Commitments to values

Great companies pick the right things to do, then do them right! The strategy designed during the past decade to make Monsanto great is in place. Certainly, there will be some adjustments — change is one of life's few constants — but the major moves have already been made. Now comes the hard task of making the strategy work. Strategy, to paraphrase management guru Peter Drucker, is worth little until it *degenerates* into work. That work must be done by the 50,000 Monsanto employees around the globe, from Argentina to Zaire. If Monsanto is to become great, it is all of us who will make it so. We have a wonderful tradition to build on. We should expect nothing less of ourselves.

The question many employees ask me these days is: What *is* the new Monsanto? What binds us together? What does Monsanto stand for as a corporation?

Let me state here and now that Monsanto is not simply a company managing a portfolio of assets. Certainly, we have given the operating units more authority to act independently — to be "self-reliant." Yet, there remains critical interaction in the form of people, corporate relationships, international skills, technology and information, and a common linkage of manipulating molecules, whether in the Chemical Company, Agricultural, Fisher, Electronics, Searle or NutraSweet.

But it takes more than strategies, businesses or molecules to bind together any superior institution. Great companies, like great people, are perceived to have a recognizable character. They are respected, admired, loved, sometimes feared. They know where they're going — that's half the battle — and they are committed to getting there. They set high goals and attain them through discipline and concentration. Above all, they are perceived to possess integrity. They do the right thing.

Monsanto is unwaveringly committed to its drive to become one of the world's great industrial enterprises. In pursuit of this goal, Monsanto will foster — indeed insist upon — high standards of behavior and operating principles across all units wherever it does business.

Our reputation — our good name — is all we have. When we go to the public for permission to operate, that reputation must be rock-solid. And we must go to the public every day in scores of ways, whether we're presenting our cases to politicians or regulators in Brussels, Brazil or Washington, D.C., or asking local communities for the right to build plants in their backyards. Indeed, I can't think of any company more dependent upon public acceptance than one operating in the chemicals, agricultural products, food and pharmaceuticals businesses.

We have moved demonstrably toward decentralization and we have prospered. Operating units thrive on independence, and we encourage that self-reliance. But we are also a family. We need a set of principles that define corporate expectations. These are broad in concept and critical in content. Adherence is unequivocal.

What we expect — indeed, demand — of the "new" Monsanto is contained in the nine principles outlined in the following categories:

- *Safety*
- *Environment and our neighbors*
- *Equal opportunity*
- *A drive for results*
- *Empowering people*
- *A global company*
- *Serving customers*
- *Doing the right thing*
- *Serving the shareowners*

These principles or commitments must be an unbreakable link among Monsanto employees — a common set of commitments that run through our decentralized company and bind us together. We will be judged by our various publics — our fellow employees, shareowners, customers and neighbors — on how we conduct ourselves. It takes years to build a reputation of integrity, but only moments to tarnish it. Once lost, a good reputation is almost impossible to restore.

These nine principles, then, are our commitments to reasserting and even improving the fine reputation that Monsanto enjoys. We are further along toward achieving some than others. But we must achieve them all, because taken together they are the prerequisites of greatness.

## Safety

The way to feel safe is to never feel secure. Monsanto's heritage in the chemical industry has taught us that safety is an obligation to both employees and neighbors. What is more, it is essential to our survival. Throughout Monsanto we handle hazardous materials and perform operations that can have disastrous consequences if adequate safety precautions are not taken. *We will create an injury-free environment for our fellow employees.*

The need for safety is most obvious in the basic chemical business, but no part of Monsanto is immune to accidents. And it's a need that goes beyond manufacturing plants and warehouses into laboratories and offices. Hands and fingers are always at risk in Fisher plants. There is the risk of spills, burns and cuts in laboratories. Searle boasts a good safety record, but no one should ever become complacent. During a visit to Skokie I was startled to discover men working at a construction site with no hard hats and scientists at their benches without safety glasses. These people were unacceptable-chance-takers, and Searle has made changes.

The Monsanto commitment to safety is as old as the company. Founder John F. Queeny learned a hard lesson when three workers inexplicably died at one of his plants. Before long, men feared to enter the plant. When it was discovered that a chemical substance was poisoning the men through their skins, Mr. Queeny immediately ordered showers installed, provided the workers with daily changes of work clothes, and changed the dusty process. Mr. Queeny learned painfully and early the need for safe processes and protection of the workers. It's a lesson Monsanto never forgot.

Subsequently, Monsanto developed one of the finest safety records in the chemical industry — an industry that today ranks as one of the safest of all.

Our safety performance began to slip a few years ago, perhaps because people's attention was diverted by the upset caused by the changes that swept Monsanto. We are recovering the lost ground. We finished 1987 with a corporate rating of 600 recordable injuries for 86,803,986 working hours. That is good, but not good enough. We must get the injury rate even lower.

Safety requires constant attention to detail. Each meeting of the Chemical Company advisory board, of which I am a member, opens with a safety report. When I visit

plants in any of our companies, the first thing I check is the safety record. During a visit to a St. Louis area plant last winter, I learned that two men had slipped on ice that day in the railyard and hurt themselves.

"Why was there ice there?" I inquired.

"Well, we just had some snow," came the answer.

That was not good enough. What if the men had been carrying hazardous material and spilled it? What if a train had been coming through that railyard?

That may sound tough, but a comparatively good safety record is *no* consolation to the employee who suffers an injury that might have been prevented. Disregard for safety is a firing offense at Monsanto, anywhere in the world. Monsanto plants around the world must operate under either local or U.S. safety standards, whichever are higher. If any employees think that we don't mean it about safety, then they might want to think about where they want to work. It won't be at Monsanto.

Keeping people safe is essential by itself, but there are sound business reasons as well for safe plants. Go into a factory anywhere in the world that has a good safety record, and you'll find a plant that enjoys high quality standards, meets commitments, and keeps costs under control. Sloppiness toward safety inevitably spills over into other activities, and the cost of business starts to rise. Over the years, I have learned that when the plants are safe, then everything else is usually right.

The drive for safety in Monsanto has no end. When we lower our employee injury rate to qualify as the industry leader we'll redouble the effort to reach zero injuries.

## Environment and our neighbors

Communities around the world are making it plain, both in word and deed, that plants operating in their neighborhood must be safe, not just for workers at the plant, but for the neighborhood as a whole. And they're right! Safety in this context can mean protection from explosions that may do damage beyond the site, but it essentially focuses upon concern over pollution of the environment around the plant — the effects of pollution of the air, the water or the land.

The pollution issue concerns the chemical and agricultural units more than the rest of Monsanto. But it is not restricted to them. Searle executives recently found themselves confronted with the problem of dealing with the pollution potential of a long-time waste disposal site for pharmaceutical byproducts. NutraSweet has reported environmental releases under a recent U.S. law.

Few incidents have so focused public attention on the dangers of chemical pollution as the deadly fallout from the accident at a plant operated by a Union Carbide subsidiary company's plant in Bhopal, India. Monsanto's response to public concern was to open our plants to public inspection, regardless of warnings that we might reveal trade secrets. Simultaneously, we conducted a high-level investigation into the potential for such a disaster at our own facilities around the world. The results of this check are programs and policies that have made manufacturing, storage and transportation of chemicals at Monsanto better and safer.

Chemical plants have traditionally been engineered to vent some of their byproducts rather than let potentially explosive pressures build up. National and local regulations permitted this practice as long as the level of emissions was harmless to people and the environment. The public is now making it clear that even these types of emissions will not be tolerated in the future.

We, with our science-based logic, may consider these demands unreasonable and unrealistic. On a cost/performance basis, we are correct. Removing the first large percentage of the polluting material can sometimes be relatively easy and inexpensive. That will remove the largest element of risk that may be present. Getting out the rest is progressively costly, especially the last 5 percent or so. But the public does not really want to know our problems. They demand a clean environment.

We have increasingly little choice but to remove that last 5 percent — or even the last 1 percent, if it proves to be unacceptable. Our neighbors say they prefer a clean environment even to jobs. Our "right to operate" and our ability to reach our goals will be available to us only as long as we come closer and closer to public expectations.

In June of 1988, we announced our policy publicly — to reduce emissions in our plants significantly, in line with public expectations. What does this mean in terms of action required? It means that the operating units' allocation of resources *must* take this into consideration. More costly process design may be the result, and some of our own growth plans may suffer in order to provide funds for the public's expectations, even where the public reacts from lack of facts. Fortunately, experience has shown that we are often able to make significant reductions at a cost we can afford.

None of this means we will submit blindly to public

pressure that we consider based on misinformation. But we have tried a decade of reasoning with the public, of explaining the risk/reward ratios and of explaining what a part per billion is and what it means. We will continue to press our case through a variety of forums. Meantime, we will proceed on the basis that we will never persuade our neighbors that they should accept any *significant* environmental risk.

We uphold high standards around the world. That's why several years ago we installed a process that removes a harmless but colored discharge at both our Muscatine, Iowa, plant and a sister plant producing the same product in Korea. I remember at that time seeing the river flowing toward our Korean plant so thick with pollutants that a person could almost walk on it. We could add nothing to make it worse. Yet we chose to eliminate the color. By the way, on my last visit to Korea I learned that the river has now been cleaned up by government order to reasonably good water quality standards. By doing what is right, Monsanto anticipated the government action.

When Monsanto closes down an operation or cleans up a waste site, we will continue to make every effort to leave the land environmentally sound. The phosphate plant we closed in Columbia, Tennessee, is an example of what must be done. There, we committed a $30 million reserve for the perpetual care of the plant site itself. We've even been planting trees to soak up the water in remaining resettling ponds. At a similar plant in Idaho, we filled in the old strip mine and replanted the surface to its original condition. Legally, we could have done less. We chose to do what we believed was right.

Being a good neighbor goes beyond running a safe, environmentally responsible plant. Monsanto people are also encouraged to give freely of their time and skills to local communities. And they do. This ranges from serving national organizations such as the United Way in the United States to contributing to local youth clubs. The vast majority of our people live relatively close to their place of work. Monsanto as a company and all of us as individuals should put something back into those communities to ensure that they are safe, attractive and culturally rich places to live and raise families. Thousands of Monsanto people meet this commitment every day. I admire them, and I'm proud of what they achieve.

The debate concerning the extent of a corporation's social responsibilities will continue to rage. But one of the hallmarks of a great company is that it takes great care to enrich the lives of its neighbors rather than merely coexisting. At the very least, it is a matter of enlightened self-interest. We belong to each community in which we operate. And it is from those communities that we must retain the right to remain in business. *We will earn that right.*

## Equal opportunity

Monsanto will be an equal opportunity employer and we will promote people equally.

We have done quite well in hiring minorities and women at the entry level of the company in the United States in recent years. But far too few have moved up to top jobs. We can point to several black or female senior executives, but in 1988, women and minorities still account for barely 4 percent of the top 500 Monsanto managers. We will do better.

The Board of Directors is pressing management to improve our record. I agree! It's the right thing to do, and it's essential to our strategy. By 1995, more than half the work force of the United States will be composed of women and minorities. In order to attract the best to

Monsanto, we need to let these workers know that they can aspire to and succeed in senior management positions. Slogans are not credible testimony; evidence that others have reached the highest level of the operating units and the corporation is the only true measure of equal opportunity. Without tapping this huge human resource, Monsanto cannot aspire to greatness as a company.

We intend to train and promote from within, but we have gone outside Monsanto to obtain top-quality, experienced women and minorities, and we will continue to do so. The availability of minorities, in the sciences particularly, remains relatively small, and minority scientists are much in demand. Monsanto is not the only company aware of national demographics and the need to hire the best people available. We're spending money to encourage minorities to seek a career in science.

But hiring alone doesn't give equal opportunity. Studies have shown that many of us carry a burden of subjective baggage about women and minorities in the workplace. For women and minorities striving to move up the corporate ladder, this can pose an enormous barrier.

Several operating units are taking steps to sensitize their managers to this issue. The Agricultural Company hired experts to conduct training sessions directed toward recognizing the uniqueness of individuals — and the capabilities that flow from that uniqueness. The Chemical Company has conducted similar programs with its senior management. We intend to continue our efforts to break down artificial barriers to success.

There is a perception in the United States that the federal government has lost interest in equal opportunity. That has caused various groups, including women and minorities, to return to the courts in an attempt to press for their own sectional advancement. *At Monsanto, we must not force people to fight their way into equal opportunity. We must give it to them as a right.*

The U.S. situation is not reflective of the world. But it is not unique either. Women are moving steadily into Monsanto work forces around the world. So, too, are minorities. Monsanto must work within the culture of each land, but we must also do what is right.

I've seen extraordinary progress in some units when managers treat equal opportunity as a wise use of human resources rather than a numbers exercise or even a social goal, as admirable as the latter may be. As with safety and environment, we will be relentless in pursuing our goals of equal opportunity and fair treatment of *all* employees. Furthermore, we will make results by managers in this area one of the more important measures of their own reward and advancement.

## A drive for results

Monsanto has had in place since the 1970s a results review process as good as any in industry. Overall, it has helped Monsanto people to focus their efforts and to achieve results. Unfortunately, a process alone doesn't guarantee success all the time. Too often, agreed-upon goals remain unmet. Worse, these failures are sometimes met with shoulder shrugs and the assignment of blame to factors beyond our control. Gyrations in energy prices is a popular excuse — or weather, or government regulations that make our life difficult.

To be fair, Monsanto's traditional dependence upon cyclical commodity businesses often did place the company at the mercy of forces outside our control. People could not be expected to control external events, so they were not always held to targets and rewarded commensurately. A corporate culture of forgiveness came into style.

It is now out of style! Monsanto has been restructured to reduce our exposure to the uncontrollable. As a company, we will be far more in control of our own "luck" — far more *makers* of conditions than *responders*. Shoulder shrugs are out of fashion. Managers and subordinates will be judged and rewarded on performance against demanding goals more than ever before. There must be a sense of urgency, a drive for results.

Make the numbers, hit the targets, get the results on time — without excuses! Looking good while missing targets is out. In Winston Churchill's words: "We are easily satisfied with the very best."

Tough language! But it is no tougher than the competitive demands that we must meet in the marketplace or in financial circles.

The last few years have shown what people can achieve when confronted with threats to their well-being. People determined to preserve their jobs manage to make their own luck. Suddenly everything gets better — attendance, product quality, customer service, the financial numbers — everything.

No one is expected to work at crisis level all the time.

In fact, the fewer crises the better. But those results show what people can achieve when they focus on a problem. We need a powerful sense of urgency to perform at our best — urgency built on pride and commitment. It should be axiomatic that when people at Monsanto agree to do something, it gets done.

It's happening all around the company. The Ag Company set out to do something about the "interminable and uncontrollable" regulatory clearance process for new products. In a recent review they told me how they intended to cut two years off the time it takes to get products cleared by regulatory agencies. In some cases, cutting two years means doubling the financial risk by doing parallel toxicology work on promising compounds. Rather than going from step 1, to 2, then to 3, they are doing the tests simultaneously. In other cases, it means picking promising candidates earlier in the commercialization process — assuming the risk of passing over candidate B or C while placing all bets on candidate A. Success in this prudent risk-taking has enormous financial rewards — two more years of precious commercial life with patent coverage. Searle is developing a similar process for its multiyear regulatory clearances.

Impatience with the status quo, a willingness to take

prudent risks, and a management willing to reward successful risk-taking are clear ingredients for a great corporation.

Ralph Waldo Emerson once remarked that "nothing great is achieved without enthusiasm." Enthusiasm has many fathers. One is being on a winning team. I have worked with units where it was a joy to participate because we saw tangible results and experienced the pride that comes with success. My favorite days were with the *Lasso* and *Roundup* herbicide businesses, managing their early

development. Others have found it with MCC's Wear-Dated Carpet, Searle's *Calan* SR hypertension drug, MAC's *Alimet* feed supplement, MCC's ABS plastics and a host of others.

The thrill of achievement goes not only to those fortunate enough to be with a clear-cut commercial winner. I see it in business turnarounds and in staff units where the people know they are good and the results show it. Results count, no matter where they are achieved. There is nothing like achieving more than you believed possible to bolster your self-image.

People find fulfillment in a variety of ways. After all, not everyone aspires to rise to the senior ranks of this or any other company. Time and again, I come across employees who truly enjoy their work and have no doubt that they are contributing to make Monsanto special. They're right.

I recently met a young man during a plant visit who was operating a *PROVOX* unit to control a chemical process. Before he had *PROVOX,* he had to go to the boss for approval or help if the slightest thing went wrong. Now he solves his own problems, partly by using the capabilities built into his interactive computer. He exuded enthusiasm and self-confidence as he showed me what he could do. As far as he was concerned, the entire plant depended upon his doing his job right. The challenge turned him on.

If you haven't enjoyed this man's experience, you have missed one of the real rewards of a career. The whole company really does depend on how well you do your job.

### Rewarding the deserving

When Charlotte McDaniel was typing this manuscript, I asked her what she thought of it. Her response was a note:

"Mr. Mahoney,

"I admire your interest in writing a book on this subject. The content at this point is informative and persuasive, and I would be inspired to challenge myself to contribute to your vision of greatness.

"One comment: Much of the talk about recognition and reward is still addressed to the upper-management level. I think you should consider fleshing out this section so that those down the organization really know you're talking to them too."

Let me set the record straight: I'm talking to everyone. Results must come from every person in the company, and rewards must flow to those who deliver — from whatever position in the company. Thanks, Charlotte.

This issue — how our careers and job performance are judged and rewarded — affects all of us. Monsanto strives to treat everyone fairly, and we will reward the deserving, but there is no question that some people feel they are passed over for advancement or pay increases even after doing good work.

Fairness is an individual perception, and it can only be achieved when people talk openly and honestly. For those of us who manage people, it means that we must level with them about their performance. Beyond that, we must say what can reasonably be expected during their career at the company. Honest appraisal is essential.

Some people say that Monsanto management talks a good game about rewarding for results, but does little about it. My knowledge of salary reviews convinces me that, more often than not, consistent individual performance has brought advancement. Even so, we are stepping up and refining our management review system. Each year, several of us at the corporate level sit down with the unit managers and review the performance and potential of several hundred employees. (The unit managers have already reviewed many more than that in preparation.)

If my experience at the corporate level is any guide, I can assure you that these appraisals focus heavily on rating the individual manager's ability both to perform against targets and to develop subordinates. I urge everyone involved in the appraisal process to follow those two guidelines. Every employee will be appraised and rewarded on performance. Managers are also expected to develop people.

To help both supervisor and subordinate talk about performance and careers, we are stepping up the rigor of the "continued employment performance appraisal" that takes place after a person has been an employee for two or three years. Too many people stay on in jobs for which they have little aptitude. They suffer, and so does Monsanto. No one likes to be let go. But it is far better for all concerned that the connection be cut earlier rather than later. Monsanto benefits, but so does the employee who escapes the emotional pain of being continually passed over for promotions. It is better that this employee be given the chance to obtain something more suited to his or her abilities. Monsanto has room for a lot of people, but it isn't the company for everyone.

Supervisors have a major role in counseling employees, but supervisors can only do so much. Employees have an equal burden. If you have high expectations, be prepared to invest personally in them. Some people who feel unfairly treated often haven't made those investments — a course that adds a new skill, a job change that broadens experience. Monsanto will never promise success as an entitlement, only as an opportunity. All of us as employees have a role to play in our success.

There is, of course, the occasional lack of "chemistry" between boss and subordinate that can get in the way of success. When that is the case, straight talk is the best solution. Initiate it if it doesn't happen fast enough for you. If straight talk fails, there are legitimate routes of appeal. But start with a fair and open self-appraisal. Make sure that you've made the personal investments that help build success.

Few people want to be on a team where everyone is rewarded alike, regardless of individual contribution. A great company must reward achievers, and we will do just that. Monsanto can help build a career, but the final responsibility for our careers lies with each of us.

Quite apart from pay and advancement, I believe Monsanto has too often shied away from public accolades for those who achieve above and beyond the call of duty. Such formal programs as the Science Awards and Master Salesman serve us well. They are significant achievements and widely acknowledged. But there are many other ways to reward achievements of less Herculean proportions. Find ways to recognize performance, and put them into place.

A new vice president at IBM once said: "I thought that it was corny and a waste of time to participate in the countless recognition 'coffees,' luncheons, dinners, personal notes, and the like — until I was honored in one of those corny and wasteful events." It is amazing how that works.

I cannot stress enough the premium we intend to place on delivering promised results, without excuse. We will recognize results:

- *in financial rewards,*
- *in promotions,*
- *in personal recognition,*
- *everywhere in the company!*

I hope that your "internal" reward system coincides with Monsanto's. When it does, the results are incredible.

## Empowering people

Every organization needs appropriate controls; otherwise, chaos exists. Fiduciary and public obligations demand that Monsanto set and maintain standards. Excessive controls, however, lead to inertia and even paralysis. Monsanto is a large company, and large companies are often slow to respond to opportunity. So we need all the flexibility we can get. People must have the freedom to do their jobs.

In addition, Monsanto no longer has a solely chemical culture derived from knowledge of and dependence upon a background in that industry. Fisher, and then Searle, brought to Monsanto totally different attitudes, practices and requirements. Thus, after these acquisitions, the various units of Monsanto no longer spoke precisely the same language.

And the switch from commodities to specialty products means Monsanto people have to be far closer to their customers than ever before. Rather than filling orders for huge amounts of "stuff" turned out by our plants and competing in price and delivery, we now have to custom-tailor products that give our customers a valuable competitive edge. That means finding out what the customers want almost before they know themselves, and then producing it better and faster than anyone else. Such intimacy and flexibility is difficult when a company is centralized. The many managerial layers impede decision-making and distort communication.

That's a prime reason why we decentralized. There were just too many levels of management between the ultimate decision-makers at the corporate level and those who actually invent, make and sell our products. Decisions that should have been made well down the line were finding their way back to St. Louis and all the way up to the corporate suite. The results often included long delays that led to missed opportunities and mistakes because communications had to pass through the hands of too many people.

We have removed at least one entire layer of management in the past few years, and in some cases more than one. Corporate staff has been reduced to the minimum required, and most staff people have been reassigned directly to the operating units. This way, operating units pay for the staff support they decide is needed. Corporate Engineering, for example, was disbanded as an entity and placed in the various operating units. Many have voiced concern that redirection of levels of management and the consequent broadening span of control will mean fewer opportunities. It certainly *does* mean fewer *bosses*.

I believe the opportunities have never been better for high-quality performers. Indeed, our analysis shows that we currently have too *few* candidates for advancement to senior positions rather than too many. And opportunity to move between units still exists to a significant degree. Beyond that, units of the size we have established — for example, a $4 billion chemical unit or a $1.5 billion agricultural unit — are bigger than most whole corporations; they provide solid internal opportunity.

The obligation of management in this environment is twofold:

> ■ *We must ensure that the job content — with fewer bosses — is more rewarding, has more freedom, more challenge.*
> ■ *We must ensure that financial rewards recognize the improved productivity. Jobs must be compensated more fully on content, implication of results, complexity and other real measures, with less emphasis on numbers managed or assets controlled.*

Corporate and unit strategy is only a blueprint. *People* make everything happen. So when we hire people, we *must* hire the best. As Edgar Queeny said half a century ago: "Pick all aces."

The responses I hear to our new idea of self-reliance for employees have been quite positive. They suggest that many people are reveling in new-found autonomy. Hourly workers in several plants are boosting productivity without needing others to tell them what to do and how to do it. More and more often, salesmen and product managers are able to do their jobs without referring to their supervisors for authorization. Those managers who have eight or 10 people reporting to them, instead of only three or four, should be too busy working on priority issues to meddle unnecessarily in the activities of their subordinates.

This story told by a Pensacola plant employee is a good illustration. He wrote to me:

"Through mid-1986, nylon tire yarn operations in Pensacola were well-entrenched in a pattern of 'maintained mediocrity.' A chronic fiber waste level of 20 percent came to be accepted as standard performance. Financial performance was marginal, at best, and Monsanto's quality image with customers was poor.

"The turning point: Late in 1986, teams of wage employees changed their jobs structures to improve quality and effectiveness. A Quality Improvement Team focused specifically on waste reduction in tire yarn.

"Sharing of tire yarn economics and the value of waste material improved everyone's understanding of the business. Employees were eager to demonstrate their ability to improve their procedures and performance. Team operators visited customer mills for a firsthand look at how yarn quality affects mill performance. The Quality Improvement Team and other employee groups each contributed to improvements. At the same time, a series of process improvements was implemented — without capital investment. The efforts of 400 employees and the process improvements are each credited with about half of the reduction in waste.

"The results: Waste levels were reduced from 21 percent to 10 percent; return on capital increased from 7 percent to 14 percent; the Total Quality Index improved from 87 to 93; conversion cost was reduced from 90 cents a pound to 69 cents; and customer complaints were reduced from 23 to 13.

"When General Tire decided to reduce the number of suppliers for nylon tire yarn, Du Pont was dropped. Monsanto became sole supplier through customer-supplier partnership and demonstrated commitment to quality."

That's *employee power*. And it has happened similarly

around Monsanto at a number of other locations under a lot of different names.

So far, so good. But there are still too many reporting points in Monsanto. And too many managers are busily "controlling down and reporting up" rather than coaching, motivating and imparting experience and knowledge to their subordinates. This holds true even at senior levels. It is equally dismaying that many are still coming to their bosses seeking approval for what is well within their authority.

Management expects this greater self-reliance to be matched by greater acceptance of accountability. And we expect this philosophy to be pushed all the way down the line. At one of my monthly lunches with Monsanto employees, a product manager reported how much more efficient he was because of his new freedom of action.

"That's great," I responded. "Are you giving similar freedom of action to the people under you?"

"No, of course not," he said. "You can't give them that sort of responsibility yet."

We can do better than that.

Monsanto people must have faith in their subordinates all the way down the line. If they don't, they either have the wrong people in the jobs, or they are failing to manage correctly.

Over the years, I have learned a few tried-and-true remedies for eliminating excessive control. Let me pass them along:

■ Establish agreed-upon performance targets. Unit targets and individual goals are essential standards at Monsanto. They must be set high if we are to achieve greatness. Employees must know what is expected of them. Then managers must get out of the way and let their people perform. Lately, I have been asking Monsanto employees if they could achieve a task relating to their job if their life depended upon it. The reply is usually: "If my life depended upon it? Sure."

Well, our livelihood does.

■ When a subordinate comes seeking permission to act, try asking: "What is the worst that can happen if this idea fails?" If you can live with the worst, then approval is generally warranted. If you can't, then the answer is no. One measure of a good manager is his or her ability to judge prudent risk versus reckless-ness. It amazes me how often control is imposed, stifling initiative, when the worst that could happen would be acceptable — and often provide a useful lesson. Supervisors should spend more time developing subordinates, and providing them with the opportunity to succeed — and, occasionally, to fail. We must grow managers, not limit them.

■ Subordinates must push their boss's patience to the limit. Don't just wait to be told what to do. Seize the initiative. Try something new. If you don't get a "no" when you ask permission to try something, then, more than likely, you have approval. Stage a little "insur-rection" now and then by questioning work that is clearly red tape and a waste of time and effort. Ask why! If you can't get satisfaction from your boss, go to your boss's boss. (Of course, you do have to be right now and then!) But those who take prudent risks and succeed will reap the rewards.

This, above all, to managers: Empower! Empower! Empower!

## A global company

Monsanto became an active participant in the world marketplace more than half a century ago. We were among the first American companies to plant international roots, with acquisitions in Wales, in the United Kingdom, in the 1920s. But we still have much more to do before we can be satisfied that our approach to business is truly global. Yet our strategy demands that it become just that, and soon.

Like most corporations over the years, we have switched back and forth between organizing our international operations around headquarters control and local control. At present, we are operating in a matrix system in which the six operating units headquartered in the United States exercise strategic control, and the four world area groups are there to help them attain their objectives.

Simply put, the *international group is organized to help the operating units make money.* When this concept is understood, it eliminates interminable discussions of lines of authority.

This structure should permit the operating units to allocate their resources more efficiently, to anticipate changing political and economic fluctuations in their various marketplaces, and to benefit from foreign technology and managerial talents.

If ever there was an area in which "neatness" doesn't count, it is in the tactics required for success in the global marketplace. There is no set formula for operating in marketplaces so culturally, politically and economically diverse as, for example, Japan, Brazil, the United Kingdom and the Soviet Union. We believe our present setup is working, but we also realize that flexibility will be required to adjust to events.

There is no such thing as a global market in which a uniform product can be sold everywhere in precisely the same manner. Individual markets differ in terms of size, regulations, product needs, financing and the like. But there is a global marketplace, and Monsanto must learn to adjust to its varied rhythms. Roberto Goizueta, chairman of Coca-Cola, advises, "Think globally, act locally."

The one constant is that Monsanto must be global if we are to become a great company. The motives vary by unit. For example, it is well understood by pharmaceutical and agricultural companies that products must be developed and sold on a worldwide basis in order to recoup the enormous R&D costs. Home country sales are seldom adequate. Customers for rubber chemicals, *Saflex* and Fisher products — the tire, automotive and petrochemical markets, respectively — are worldwide, and expect worldwide service from their suppliers. Other parts of the company have equally urgent reasons to sell to the world.

But saying we're global isn't enough. At a lunch recently, a young woman who deals with international shipping in a product group made the point well: "Of

course, we only get our shipments after the U.S. customers have been taken care of." I suggested that maybe her own international customers were infrequent users, or simply international price shoppers. "Not at all — they've been my customers for years," she said, "and they still come second with the people who make the decisions." That is *not* global thinking.

Fortunately, I hear much more talk these days about global markets from our product people. There are still a few product groups that have as their international policy "when and if we get around to it." But that's becoming rarer, because it's a recipe for global failure. Increasingly, across the company there is a true sense of how critical the development, care and attention to global business is to Monsanto's success.

In time, if we do our job right, we estimate that Monsanto's total business will be split roughly 50-50 between the United States and international markets. But it won't come by default.

The obvious corollary to increased international importance is that more Monsanto managers must gain personal international experience. And that does not just mean heading off on one of those one- or two-week trips without specific objectives, just "to see what's going on," that waste money and drive our international local managers to distraction. We don't need that kind of "experience."

Increased international experience also doesn't necessarily mean "a three-year stint in London or Brussels." Europe is a vital market for Monsanto and will increasingly be so, as the Common Market continues to evolve into a unified economic unit. But Latin America, Asia and the Eastern Bloc countries are also of great importance. The Pacific Basin area, for example, has been the fastest-growing economic sector in the world for a decade, and this pace seems likely to continue.

We must, therefore, grow a cadre of executives comfortable with dealing across the world scene. Not all international assignments necessarily require foreign postings, but many will. The operating units have begun posting *senior* U.S. executives abroad to broaden their experience. Conversely, more non-U.S. citizens will move into key spots in the United States. And nowhere is it written that the chief executive officer of Monsanto must be an American.

Not surprisingly, then, a more multinational Monsanto means that international assignments will increase in number and figure more importantly in career advancements than ever before. I was given an important international responsibility at a crucial time in my career, and I can attest that it taught me never again to think about the business without considering the worldwide implications.

## Serving customers

My colleague Earle Harbison used to remark that we were once a company "that manufactured products we then had to sell." He was not being altogether facetious. Back then, we turned out huge volumes of commodities and enticed customers into buying them on the basis of price, delivery and some service. We were good at it, and it paid us well. But we spent limited time worrying about the needs of our customers. When they said, "Send us some stuff," we obliged. In the jargon of business, we were product-driven, and that met the needs of the time.

Today, we are largely in the business of selling products that we term value-added. We add as much value as possible to the raw materials and charge for that technological addition. But customers don't really care about value added; all they care about is value *received*. And value received from our customers' point of view is the special something that gives them a distinctive edge over their competition. To gain that edge, they will pay well, as we saw when *NutraSweet* sweetener contributed to making Diet Coke and Diet Pepsi the fastest-growing products in their markets.

Monsanto's primary purpose is to discover what we can make that the marketplace will pay handsomely for. That's why Monsanto managers are spending hours with customers — whether soft-drink manufacturers, automakers, soap makers, doctors or farmers — trying to learn what they need and how we can provide it. We will have products in the right place, at the right time and for the right price. Fortunately, customers who once kept us at arm's length to protect their trade secrets and bargaining leverage now increasingly welcome such collaborations. Value added *can* become value received.

The traditional chemical segments of Monsanto are going a step further and are dealing with a customer they once met only rarely — the consumer of products at retail. Take the success of *StainBlocker,* our stain-resistant nylon fiber that has given an enormous boost to carpet sales across the United States. *StainBlocker* resulted from Monsanto's listening to homeowners. Americans were happy with the styles and colors of carpeting on the market. But our market research showed that for $20 or $30 a square yard, they wanted something that would not be ruined by every spilled glass of juice or coffee. Our research people came up with *StainBlocker* — an enormous commercial success.

This focus upon the customer must penetrate deep into the Monsanto consciousness, far beyond those front-line troops, the salesmen and marketers. Our annual research bill now tops $600 million. That is more than we spend on capital investments. The purpose of this research is to provide leads for exciting new products for Monsanto to sell. Monsanto scientists need to ensure that their research is moving toward that end. I tell our researchers regularly, "Leave that bench now and then and go to lunch with a marketer. Visit customers and find out what they want or what they *should* want." An alternative is to get marketing people excited about something research is working on that seems to have product potential. Either way, marketing and research are two sides of the same coin — providing products for customers. They must talk to the customers — and to each other.

Plant employees at all levels also must focus on customers who not only want product at the right price and on time, but want it to perform as advertised. Every time! They want quality. Quality in terms of manufacture, quality in terms of delivery, quality in terms of backup service. Certainly, price is a vital ingredient, but nobody buys on price alone. Look below the price equation and you will invariably find that the real measure is whether the product does what is promised and does it consistently. If it does that, the customer will keep your plant in business.

Product quality is one of my special interests. Back in my days in plastic products, we experimented with manufacturing doormats. To test the ability of these mats to survive severe winters, we stored them in an icehouse for hours and then slammed them against a concrete post. When the mats could survive what was called "the 10 Mahoney whacks" test, we knew they were ready for the marketplace. That's not very sophisticated, but it worked. And quality works every time.

We must get our products out into the world as soon as possible, and cut and fit them to the demands of the marketplace. But we must make equally sure we don't go foisting off inferior products. Nothing should anger us more than seeing either the Monsanto imprimatur or a valued brand name attached to an inferior product.

We should also strive for worldwide consistency of quality. Not long ago, the rubber chemicals group came up with a product designed to compete in Europe against a similar product made by a respected European competitor. It did well. Some time later, I saw the version of the product we planned to market in the United States.

"It's not as good as the stuff we make in Europe," I remarked to the product manager.

"It's a hell of a lot better than it was!" he replied.

"Maybe," I said, "but that's still not good enough." And as it turned out, it wasn't. Now it is.

Historically, Monsanto's product reputation with its customers has been good, but not always "great." Some customers grant an "automatic sheen" to Monsanto products, and the number is increasing. We have dramatically raised the quality of some of those products that were lagging in quality — *Saflex* and silicon wafers, to name just two of many major quality improvements. But there is always room to improve. That's essential, because our competitors have recognized the importance of quality too. We must stay ahead.

Quality not only sells, it also creates pride. At a recent employee lunch I was describing how the name *Simplesse* had been chosen for that NutraSweet product, and I explained that it would be used in such edibles as ice cream.

"Why *Simplesse?*" asked my interrogator. "Why not use our own name?"

"Monsanto ice cream?" I wondered, thinking of con-

sumer response to an "all natural" ice cream bearing the
name of a company perceived to be in the chemical
business.

"Why not?" came the response. "If we're proud of our
name."

My luncheon guest may not have been a consumer
marketing man. And then, it's a NutraSweet product, so
NutraSweet picked the name. But I like his instincts and
attitude. We should be proud enough of every product
we make to put our name on it. The Monsanto or Monsanto affiliate's name should be our customers' guarantee
of quality. Programs like the Chemical Company's
Total Quality and MAC Quality are making that happen.
We need all we can get.

I hope that no one in the entire Monsanto Company
ever forgets Henry Ford's words: "It's not the employer
who pays the wages — he only handles the money. It is
the product that pays the wages." Our products must serve
our customers well.

## Doing the right thing

There is no right way to do a wrong thing. In 26 years
with this company, I have never been asked — nor have

I felt expected — to do anything that I would be ashamed of in getting my job done. Nor have I seen it take place around me at Monsanto. "Doing the right thing" is deeply ingrained in the Monsanto culture. I believe that we are *already* a great company in this respect.

Founder John Queeny set the tone when the company was on the verge of bankruptcy in the early days. His aides suggested that they close down the plant, lay off all the workers, and then open up with new people, at lower wages. "Since when," replied Mr. Queeny, "do we lie to our employees?"

Under Mr. Queeny, Monsanto emerged as an industrial leader in such matters as worker safety, paid vacations, benefits, pensions, bonuses, even a stock purchase plan for employees — unusual for that time. The founder also instituted a no-layoff policy during the Great Depression in the 1930s.

The tradition of caring about employees continued. Mr. Queeny's son, Edgar, was at the helm of the company several years later, when a freighter exploded in the harbor at Texas City and destroyed the nearby Monsanto plant. Edgar Queeny flew to the disaster site and handed out cash to the families of the nearly 300 employees injured. The money enabled them to take care of immediate needs with no red tape while they awaited insurance claims. In its time, the gesture was substantial, and it was never forgotten by the families affected. He simply felt it was "the right thing to do."

When asked for his prime requisite in an employee, John Queeny replied: "Character."

People of character do the right thing. It is bred in the bone.

Monsanto comprises people from all over the world, from a wide variety of cultures and backgrounds. We operate in countries where the ethics of the society and the business community often differ one from another. Yet I believe that people everywhere understand what is meant by "doing the right thing." People know character, and Monsanto people have it.

Whenever a company sets financial standards that are tough to reach, it runs the risk that some people will succumb to the pressure and act unethically to meet their targets. Years ago, I knew a fellow — a district sales manager who worked for another company — who was doing things I thought unacceptable. I asked him why. "I want to get promoted," he said. He made all his targets, but he got fired when his employer learned his methods. The company he worked for would not put up with it. Neither will Monsanto.

If you ever feel pressure to act in a way that violates

ethical standards, refuse to cave in to it. If you are asked directly to act unethically and you cannot resolve the matter with your boss or your boss's boss, then bring it to my attention. Like safety, this is a nonnegotiable issue at Monsanto.

Mr. Queeny set the standard. It has been constant through the years. We shall not tarnish it.

## Serving the shareowners

The lofty goals Monsanto has set for its employees, retirees, its neighbors — indeed for our own long-term survivability — cannot be satisfied unless our owners are satisfied.

Earlier, I described maximizing shareowner values as the *enabler* that makes all the "great company" attributes possible. The links among our many constituencies cannot be separated. In my letter to the shareowners in 1987, I wrote: "We can serve our shareowners well only when we have served our customers well, when our people are highly innovative and productive and, in our mix of chemical-related businesses, when our neighbors and those who act for them grant us the right to operate."

In the early days of Monsanto, it was easy to identify

and serve the shareowners — the Queenys. The early records of their writings show they knew well the linkage among all the stake holders. Today, Monsanto shareowners seemingly have varied interests. The financial institutions that hold the bulk of our shares move in and out of our stock depending on its behavior at any given time. Indeed, at one time recently, our biggest shareowner was a computer-driven fund that bought and sold shares on the basis of programmed dividend information. Monsanto is, in fact, an active and popular trading stock. Each share of Monsanto stock traded the equivalent of 1.25 times in 1987.

In this environment, it is perhaps a difficult rallying point to aim our actions at "serving the shareowners." They are no longer the Queenys. Our owners are dispassionate — but hardly disinterested in everything we do.

There is little sentiment involved among institutional investors. Nevertheless, our major institutional holders — while they buy and sell daily — tend to stay with us over time. These so-called "in-and-out, short-term" investors often turn out in reality to be long-term investors with a vital interest in our fortunes.

A number of financial market analysts have supported us for years — staking their own reputations on their belief in our strategy. When I meet with them and with the portfolio managers who make the buy and sell decisions, they tend to be interested in the same thing we as employees are interested in — making Monsanto the best it can be. True, they have less patience for the promise of reward "sometime in the '90s." They want us strong in the long term — but also want regular rewards between now and then. There should be no conflict between what they want and what we deliver. Our major owners *are* our owners, and have the rights of ownership. They want to balance short- *and* long-term rewards. Consistently disappointing them in the near term will inevitably cause them to lose faith in the long term — and they will drop their support. That has potentially disastrous results, as many companies with depressed stock prices have found, to their dismay.

Our owners will permit — indeed, welcome and support — our long-term strength, provided we meet our promised targets on a regular and consistent basis.

We are proceeding consciously and deliberately to report steady, reliable, year-by-year financial gains. But everything is a balance, and the philosophy of building the long-term values that will make this a great company will not be undermined by short-term expediency. Fortunately, our experience has shown us that both long- and short-term targets can be achieved. And they must be.

The result of our performance in 1987 was a return on shareholders' equity that is little more than half the 20 percent figure established as the target of financially great companies. MCC and MAC are meeting those targets. NutraSweet is close (while being measured somewhat differently). Fisher and Monsanto Electronic Materials Company have a long way to go. Searle is on its planned path, but still needs "the numbers." All performances are improving significantly in 1988 and are expected to continue to improve, year by year, as we move forward.

Ironically, steadily growing earnings make it difficult to boost the corporate return-on-equity (ROE) figure when those earnings are retained within the corporation. Retained earnings at Monsanto were increasing shareholders' equity to the extent that, when we opened the doors every January 1, Monsanto had to generate an additional $25 million or so in new income just to "stay in place" in terms of the critical measure of return on shareowners' equity. The company therefore decided to ease this burden, at least for the near term, by buying back Monsanto shares at a rate designed to keep shareholders' equity constant and to increase our returns on that shareowner investment by our earnings gains.

We're making excellent progress, but we still have a way to go to achieve great financial earnings. Each year we will have to do markedly better than the year before. This will require both annual and long-term discipline.

There will be changes in tactics — making acquisitions or taking new product directions, removing businesses that constantly perform poorly — as we move toward that 20 percent ROE goal. But the fundamental strategy will not change. Management is committed to financial superiority and all the great things that it brings to the various stake holders of Monsanto.

"The reputation
of a person is
like his shadow:
It sometimes
follows and sometimes
precedes him.
It is sometimes
longer and sometimes
shorter than
his normal size."

French Proverb

# The fruits of greatness

The strategy is working. The financial results are improving. New products are on the way and old ones are taking on renewed life. Morale is picking up around the company. Many people tell me that the new-found freedom from corporate control among operations is allowing them to contribute to the enterprise as never before. We are on our way to greatness, by every measure.

How will we know when we arrive?

The most identifiable — but by no means the only — measure of greatness will be the elevation of Monsanto's financial results into that rarefied atmosphere of 20 percent return on shareowners' equity and a 10 percent annual increase in earnings.

We'll also be able to measure some of the other major commitments — a better safety record, significantly lower environmental emissions, more women and minorities in the work force, more quality accolades from customers. But the greatest measure will be intangible — the pride we all feel when working for a great company. Superb financial results should be seen more as a means than as an end. They will enable us to have the time and opportunity to achieve greatness in the eyes of all our stake holders, whatever the nature of their particular stake. Monsanto will merit the title "great" when we fully use that most potent of our assets — the 50,000 men and women who come to work each day in our plants and offices around the globe.

So what are the benefits of greatness?

Let me start with those that flow most directly from superior financial results. Superior results boost the price of Monsanto stock. That naturally pleases the share-owners — both external and internal. But it also gives Monsanto the wherewithal to make corporate acquisitions for less, and that avoids piling up mountains of debt. Importantly, a strong share price reduces the likelihood that Monsanto will be a takeover target — no small consideration in these days of raiders and corporate takeovers.

Stronger financial results benefit Monsanto across the board. They supply cash that can be plowed into our R&D drive to renew existing products and to create new ones. They permit us to hire the best people, to improve our workplace and to remove as much drudgery as possible from our jobs. They allow pay for performance at all levels. They allow Monsanto to take a leadership role in the communities in which we operate and live.

We have run Monsanto with and without good income levels in recent years. *With* is better! For everyone.

But let me go beyond the direct financial results to other

rewards of great companies. Recognized corporate superiority serves as an invaluable *selling tool*. Just think how
pleasant it was for IBM salesmen to make a call back in
the days when their company was synonymous with the
computer industry. When they went in to see customers,
they were backed by a huge competitive advantage. I know
just how much fun the job can be when you have that edge.
Back when *Roundup* was introduced as *the* herbicide, I had
to inform a Japanese businessman and his assembled
executives that their company would not be selected as a
distributor of *Roundup*. Later, the businessman remarked
that the loss of face was so substantial that in an earlier
time he would have had to resign. I regretted causing him
embarrassment, but the sensation of possessing so valued
a product was exhilarating.

The customer lets you know when your product is king.
It is a wonderful feeling.

The competitive edge goes beyond customers. A variety of institutions come to hold you in high esteem. Top
universities approach you about cooperating on advanced
research projects, and their graduates want to come work
for you. Government authorities and politicians request
the company's opinion on matters before them and pay
attention to the answers. The national media broadcast
your company's success. And regulators processing your

submissions for product approvals around the world are not immune to reputation — good or bad.

A quality reputation is equally valuable in times of trouble. Great companies get the benefit of the doubt, at least once. Johnson & Johnson, for example, survived a potentially damaging experience with poisoned Tylenol, their market-leading analgesic. The company handled itself well, *but* an important factor in their recovery was the public's belief that J&J was a quality company that could be trusted to solve the problem.

Fortunately, Monsanto already scores quite well on that sort of trust. Recently, when the U.S. Food and Drug Administration expressed irritation at the way Nutra-Sweet announced *Simplesse,* without seeking their explicit approval, financial analysts called with concerns about the product and its future. Those concerns could have lowered the price of our stock. They listened to us, and were reassured. Wall Street may not have given Nutra-Sweet high marks for diplomacy, but the analysts believed that if a Monsanto subsidiary said *Simplesse* was safe, then it was. Monsanto, they were saying, can be trusted on that sort of thing.

The competitive edge that comes from working on a winner is matched by personal rewards that might best be defined as the sense of self-worth. Winning is the great motivator, and people who contribute to victories grow in self-confidence and self-esteem. During the early days of the Agricultural Company successes, I saw dozens of people grow into world-beaters because they were contributing to a winner.

No product can be a winner all the time. And there is nothing so debilitating as working on a product that has hopeless prospects. That is partly why we chose to get out of such businesses during our restructuring. But there

are products on the decline that can be turned around by imagination and initiative. Look at the way the chemical group has revitalized 50-year-old *Saflex,* the way the agricultural group has developed new market opportunities for *Roundup,* and the way Searle has renewed *Calan.* Look at the excitement and success at Pensacola, Decatur and Nitro, where employees have revitalized their plants. There is great excitement and stimulation to be had from transforming an apparent decliner into a winner. Like it or not, many of us perform better under this kind of pressure. Of course, we can't and shouldn't operate regularly in a crisis mode — but we *can* bring the spirit, sense of purpose, initiative and pride of success we so often see in a crisis to our "business as usual."

Only in the past century or so has work been regarded as a potentially ennobling activity that can bring psychic rewards. Many people may still regard it as a necessary evil. But it need not be. After all, we devote most of our waking hours to our job — traveling to and from it, doing it, and thinking about it. So why not work at making the job an activity that is enjoyable, or at least fulfilling? Decentralization has the potential to give Monsanto people at all levels more control over their jobs by reducing the bureaucracy and managerial interference. The increased interaction with customers has brought greater diversity to most jobs. I urge all of you to seize these opportunities for initiative and to act upon them.

In a society that has seen the splintering of so many traditional bonds, the place where we work has become increasingly important in defining who we are and what we stand for. People who work for companies perceived to be superior in purpose and achievement share some of that aura. This is especially true in smaller communities around the world, where the Monsanto operations are often leading employers and contributors of time, talent and funds to the enrichment of city and town.

The most moving aspect of any Monsanto retirement function is to hear long-time employees tell how solid a strand the company has been in the fabric of their lives. These are not necessarily people who climbed high upon the career ladder, but men and women who made successes of their time at Monsanto. Weekends and vacations are too short to be the total focus of life's fulfillment.

★ ★ ★ ★

But change happens. Even world-class teams age and fall to the bottom of the standings unless they are regularly renewed by wise trades and draft choices. The same is true with companies and products. There was a time, not all that long ago, when most companies never dropped businesses. They just kept them going in hopes that, with time and effort, they would recover one day. International competition and the corporate raiders changed all that. Now businesses must pull their weight or go.

Monsanto will always be dropping businesses at the bottom and adding new ones at the top. The Chemical unit, for example, is short of major new products to replace winners that someday will move to the end of their life cycle. That is why we will invest seed money in chemically targeted venture capital funds to search out and develop new specialty products.

While this kind of renewal will always take place, the major, strategic changes at Monsanto have been made. We have a good product mix in the new Monsanto. The products of the old Monsanto are performing superbly. In the new additions to the company, NutraSweet is providing a steady stream of cash — and showing promising new products. R&D investments are beginning to bear fruit at Searle. We are even well set to avoid the worst ravages of economic recession.

Monsanto will be an exciting, stimulating place to work

and to build a career. I come to work every morning — well, almost every morning — eager to tackle the challenges of the day. I hope you do too. There will be more than enough challenges for all of us in the years ahead. We need your skills and your commitment. I see in my mind 50,000 Monsanto people around the world sharing a dream for the company and breaking down the doors to get to work each day to join in. Blue sky? Perhaps. But just imagine it happening. There would be no limit to what we could achieve.

"Let each

of

you

find where

your

chance

for

greatness

lies."

from *Chariots of Fire*

# Final thoughts

P olicy is what we do, not what we say. That is why commitment to the principles in this book must be embodied in all our actions. They must be second nature to us all, part of our daily routine — not something we have to think about or consider. It takes that kind of consistent effort to be great. We are already there in some areas. We have our work cut out for us in others. In every case, there can be no going back. Each principle must become our policy *in fact* if we are to achieve the goals set out for Monsanto — and if our people are to prosper.

Think about these principles! Talk about them! Live them every day at work! I'm committed to helping you turn them into action. And it will take all of you — all of us — working together to fulfill our vision and to live our dream. I want all of us to benefit from the pride that comes from working for a company that stands for — *and delivers* — greatness.